Contents

Creative origami crafts

Well-folded origami models are treasures all by themselves. But when you place them on greetings cards, hang them on strings or feature them on scrapbook pages, your tiny paper creations become masterpieces! Send a friend a delightful origami duck pond greetings card. Transform origami cubes into glowing paper lanterns. Make origami photo frames into perfect keepsake ornaments. With the models in this book, there are no limits to the origami crafts you can create!

Download the 4D app!

Videos for every fold and craft are now at your fingertips with the 4D app.

To download the 4D app:
- Search in the Apple App Store or Google Play for "Capstone 4D"
- Click *Install* (Android) or *Get*, then *Install* (Apple)
- Open the application
- Scan any page with this icon

You can also access the additional resources for each chapter on the web at **www.capstone4D.com** using the password **fold.origami**

Materials

Origami is great for crafting because the materials don't cost much. Below are the basic supplies you'll use to complete the projects in this book.

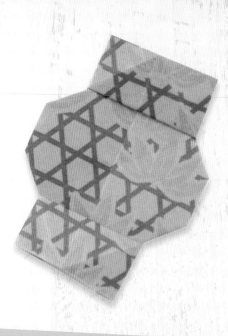

origami paper

scissors

markers

coloured paper

clothes pegs

beads

coloured card stock

sewing needle

yarn

glue sticks

self-adhesive gemstones

string

hot glue

photos

wire

craft glue

LED lights

ribbon

double-sided tape

magnets

sweets

Terms and techniques

Folding paper is easier when you understand basic origami folding terms and symbols. Practise the folds below before trying the models in this book.

Valley folds are represented by a dashed line. One side of the paper is folded against the other like a book.

Mountain folds are represented by a dashed and dotted line. The paper is folded sharply behind the model.

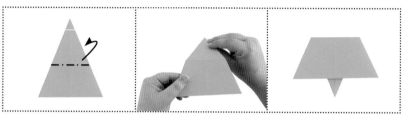

Squash folds are formed by lifting one edge of a pocket. The pocket gets folded again so the spine gets flattened. The existing fold lines become new edges.

Inside reverse folds are made by opening a pocket slightly. Then you fold the model inside itself along the fold lines or existing creases.

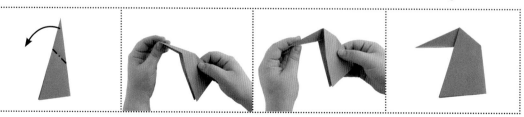

Outside reverse folds are made by opening a pocket slightly. Then you fold the model outside itself along the fold lines or existing creases.

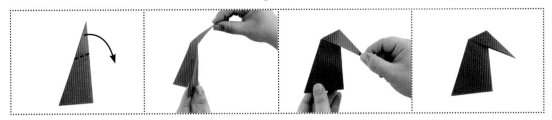

Rabbit ear folds are formed by bringing two edges of a point together using existing fold lines. The new point is folded to one side.

Pleat folds are made by using both a mountain fold and a valley fold.

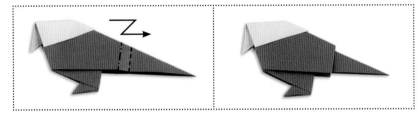

Symbols

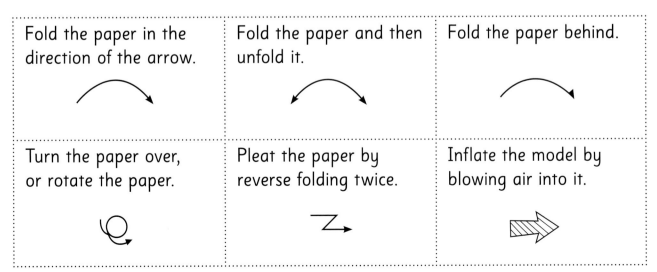

Fold the paper in the direction of the arrow.	Fold the paper and then unfold it.	Fold the paper behind.
Turn the paper over, or rotate the paper.	Pleat the paper by reverse folding twice.	Inflate the model by blowing air into it.

Origami greetings cards

 # Hen

Here's a rare origami model that uses the white side of the paper for its main colour. This hen only needs a flash of red to proudly strut her stuff.

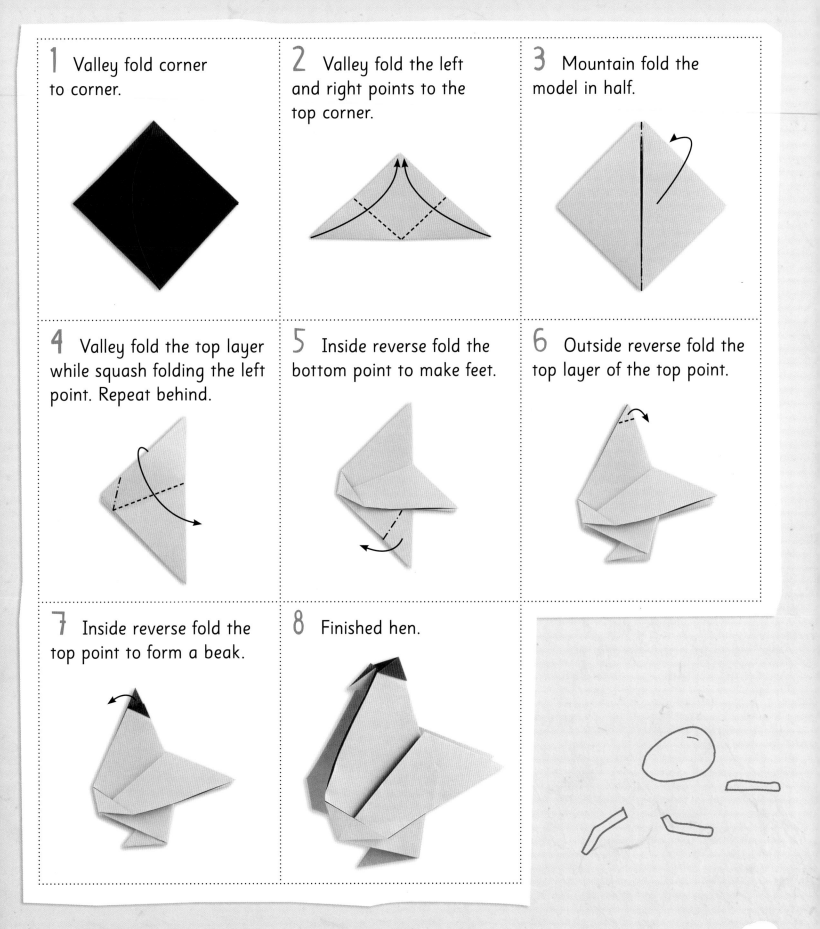

1 Valley fold corner to corner.

2 Valley fold the left and right points to the top corner.

3 Mountain fold the model in half.

4 Valley fold the top layer while squash folding the left point. Repeat behind.

5 Inside reverse fold the bottom point to make feet.

6 Outside reverse fold the top layer of the top point.

7 Inside reverse fold the top point to form a beak.

8 Finished hen.

Pig

With its little snout and tail, there is only one way to make this paper porker cuter. Fold it in pretty pink or peach paper.

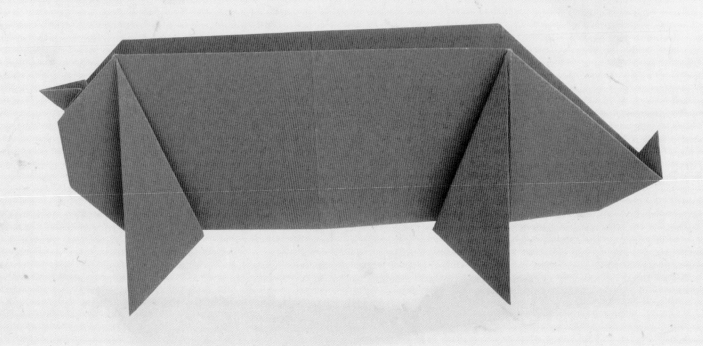

1 Valley fold edge to edge in both directions and unfold.

2 Valley fold the edges to the centre.

3 Valley fold the edges to the centre and unfold.

4 Valley fold the corners to the creases made in step 3 and unfold.

5 Squash fold the corners on the existing creases.

6 Mountain fold the model in half.

7 Valley fold the inside points to the vertical creases. Repeat behind.

8 Inside reverse fold the point to start the tail.

9 Inside reverse fold the hidden point to make the tip of the tail.

10 Mountain fold the top layer of the point to round the rump. Repeat behind.

11 Inside reverse fold the point to make the snout.

12 Finished pig.

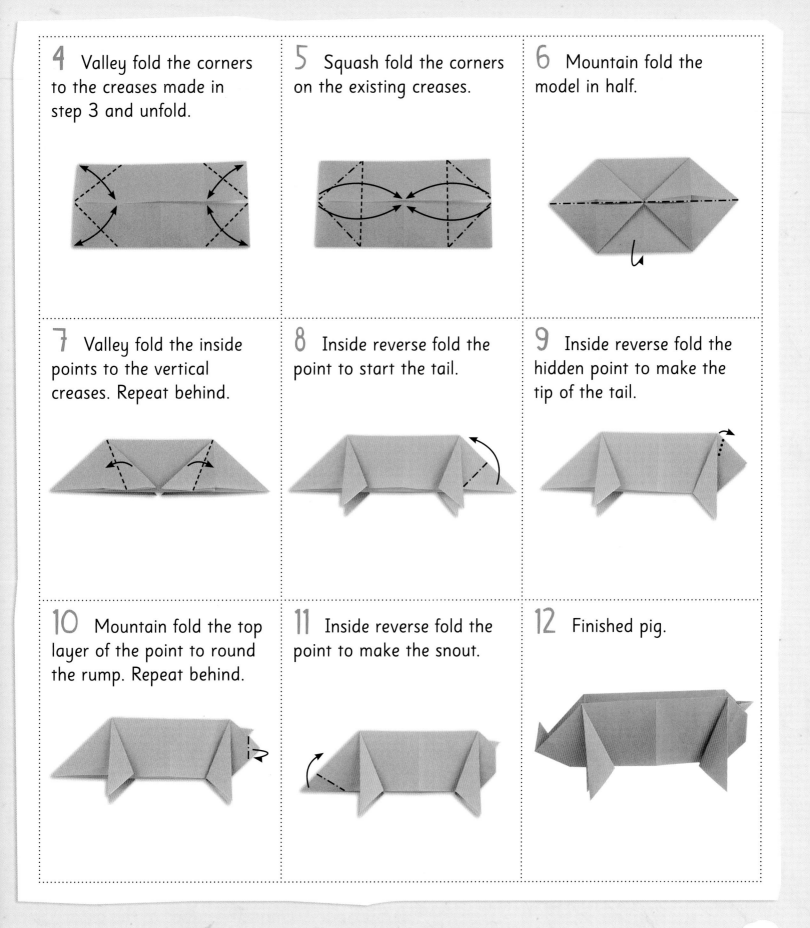

Barnyard card

Build a barnyard card that would make Old MacDonald proud. It's the perfect setting for your origami pigs and hens.

What you need

22- by 28-centimetre (8.5- by 11-inch) sheet of red card stock

scissors

double-sided tape

13 15-cm (6-in.) strips of white card stock

2- by 2.5-cm (0.75- by 1-in.) piece of red card stock

2.5- by 3.2-cm (1- by 1.25-in.) piece of white card stock

large origami hen

3 small origami hens

2 origami pigs

*fold the pigs and large hen from 10.2-cm (4-in.) squares, and the small hens from 7.6-cm (3-in.) squares

What you do

1 Fold the red sheet of card stock in half so the long edges meet. Unfold.

2 Cut the card stock in half along the crease made in step 1. Put one half to one side.

3 Fold the piece of card stock you kept in half so the short edges meet. Unfold.

4 Fold the sides of the card stock to the crease made in step 3. Put the doors of your barn to one side.

5 Pick up the other piece of card stock you put to one side in step 2. Cut out a barn roof shape. Make the base of the roof wide enough to match the width of the doors.

6 Tape the doors to the base of the roof.

7 Tape strips of white card stock around the edges of the doors and roof. Trim off any extra strips that extend beyond the edges of the card.

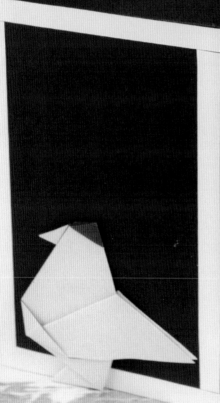

8 Tape the small red rectangle of
card stock on top of the slightly
larger white rectangle of card
stock. Tape this small door
to the barn's roof.

9 Tape the origami hens and
pigs anywhere you like inside
and outside the barn to
complete your card.

Teacup

Tea plays an important role in Japanese culture. This model represents the simple beauty of a traditional teacup.

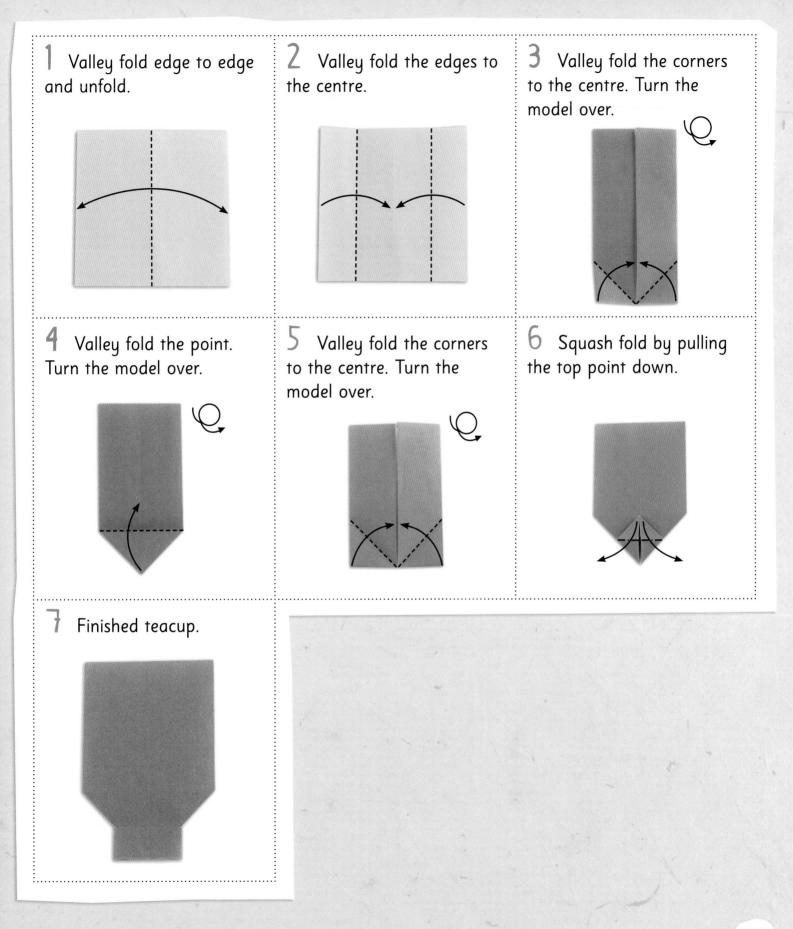

1 Valley fold edge to edge and unfold.

2 Valley fold the edges to the centre.

3 Valley fold the corners to the centre. Turn the model over.

4 Valley fold the point. Turn the model over.

5 Valley fold the corners to the centre. Turn the model over.

6 Squash fold by pulling the top point down.

7 Finished teacup.

Paper lantern

In Japan and China, paper lanterns often light up celebrations and festivals. They are also hung outside businesses to attract customers.

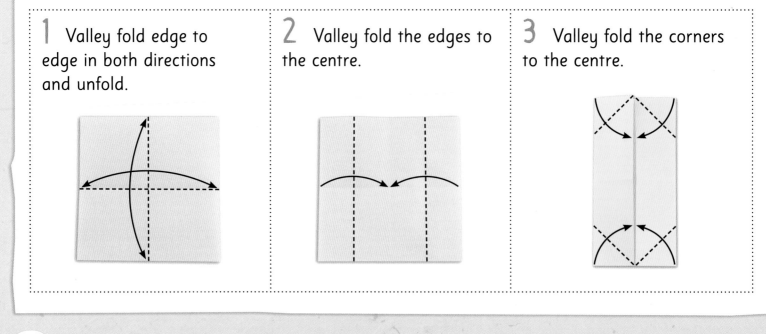

1 Valley fold edge to edge in both directions and unfold.

2 Valley fold the edges to the centre.

3 Valley fold the corners to the centre.

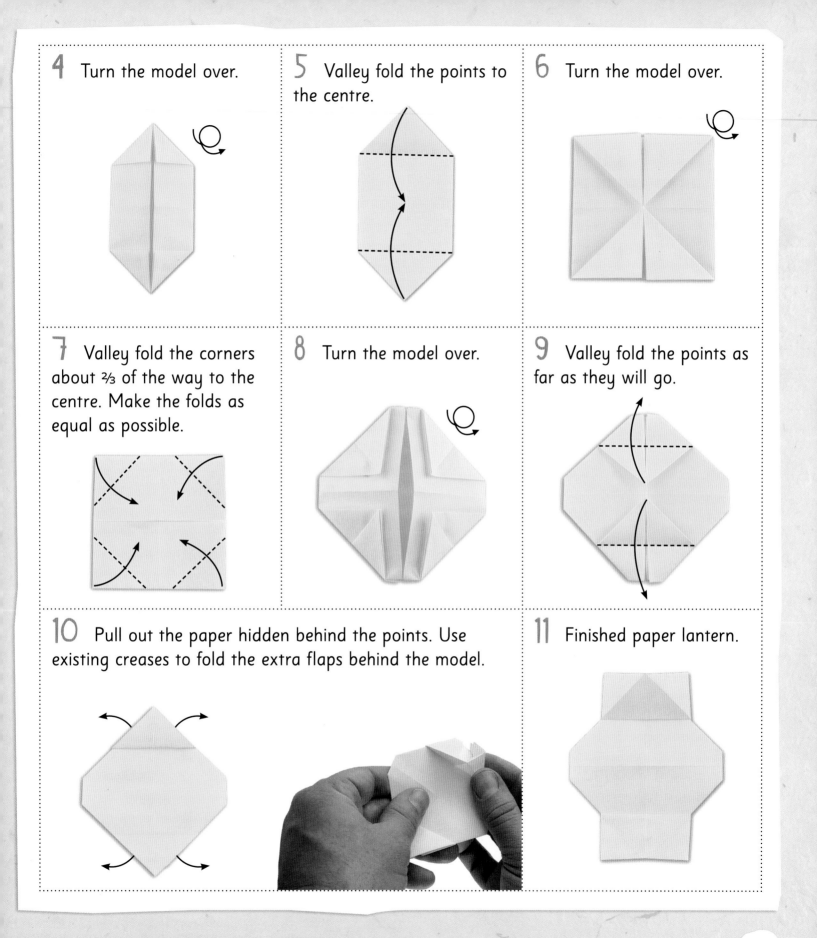

4 Turn the model over.

5 Valley fold the points to the centre.

6 Turn the model over.

7 Valley fold the corners about ⅔ of the way to the centre. Make the folds as equal as possible.

8 Turn the model over.

9 Valley fold the points as far as they will go.

10 Pull out the paper hidden behind the points. Use existing creases to fold the extra flaps behind the model.

11 Finished paper lantern.

Tea shop card

Make origami greetings cards that burst with surprises! Use origami lanterns and teacups to create an amazing pop-up tea shop card.

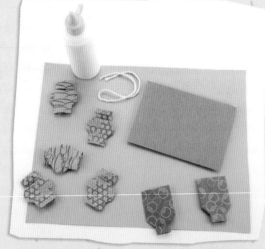

What you need

21.6- by 28-cm (8.5- by 11-in.) sheet of green card stock

15- by 9-cm (6- by 3.5-in.) piece of brown card stock

craft glue

2 origami teacups

5 origami lanterns

21.6-cm (8.5-in.) long piece of yarn

*fold the teacups and lanterns from 7.6-cm (3-in.) squares

What you do

1 Fold the green sheet of card stock in half so the short edges meet. Put the card to one side.

2 Fold narrow flaps on both short edges of the brown piece of card stock. Then fold the piece of card stock in half so the flaps meet. This will be your pop-up table.

3 Glue the flaps of the pop-up table inside the card so the table folds and unfolds when the card is opened and closed. Be sure to line up the bottom of the table with the bottom edge of the card. Allow to dry.

4 Glue a small origami teacup to each side of the table. Allow to dry.

5 Glue the paper lanterns along the length of the yarn. Allow to dry.

6 Glue the string of paper lanterns inside the card so it hangs above the table when the card is opened. Allow to dry.

Mandarin duck

The male mandarin duck is known for the "sail" feathers that stick up from his back. This model uses that feature to create a truly unique origami duck.

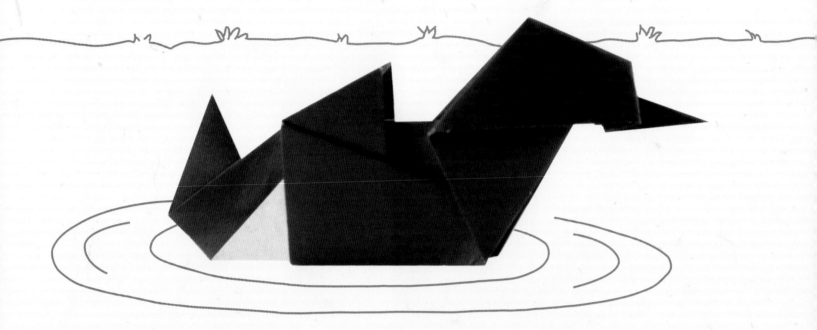

1 Valley fold corner to corner and unfold.

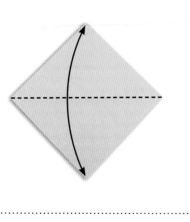

2 Valley fold the edges to the centre. Turn the model over.

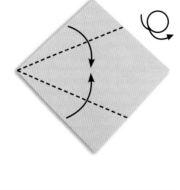

3 Valley fold the right corner about ¾ of the way to the left point.

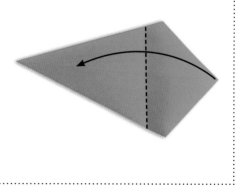

4 Valley fold the top flap along the vertical edge.

5 Mountain fold the model in half.

6 Valley fold the top layer so the dot meets the top edge. Repeat behind.

7 Outside reverse fold so the dot meets the top edge.

8 Outside reverse fold the point to make the head.

9 Pleat fold the head to make the beak.

10 Pleat fold the point to make a tail.

11 Finished mandarin duck.

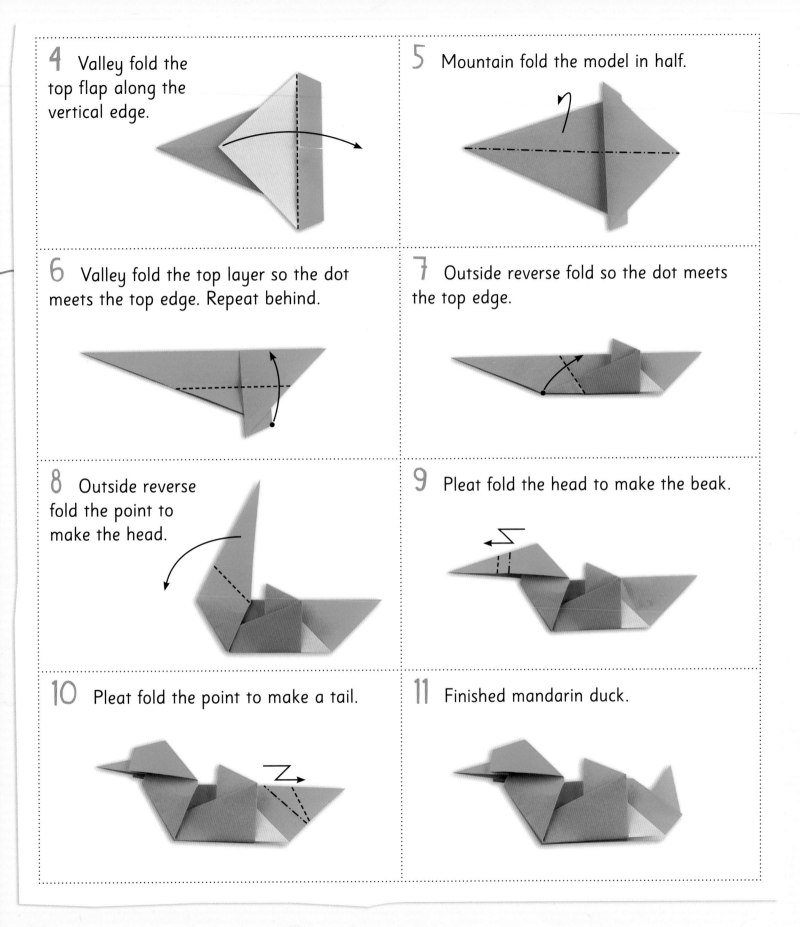

Duck pond card

Delight your loved ones with this origami duck pond card.
It's perfect for thank-you notes or invitations to an outdoor party.

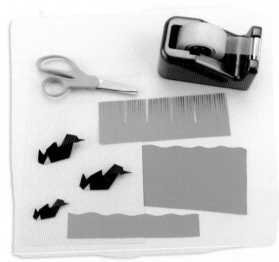

What you need

14- by 19-cm (5.5- by 7.5-in.)
   piece of tan card stock

scissors

5- by 14-cm (2- by 5.5-in.) piece
   of green paper

double-sided tape

7.6- by 14-cm (3- by 5.5-in.) piece
   of blue paper

4- by 14-cm (1.5- by 5.5-in.) piece
   of blue paper

2 large origami ducks

small origami duck

*fold the large ducks from 10.2-cm
   (4-in.) squares, and the small duck
   from a 7.6-cm (3-in.) square

What you do

1 Fold the tan piece of card stock in half
   so the short edges meet. Put the card to
   one side.

2 Cut narrow slits all along one long edge
   of the green paper to make grass. Each
   slit should be about 2.5 centimetres
   (1 inch) deep.

3 Tape the green paper to the card. Make
   the top of the grass even with the folded
   edge of the card.

4 Cut a wavy line along one long edge
   of the large blue paper. Make your cut
   about 1.3 centimetres (0.5 inch) in from
   the edge.

5 Tape the large blue paper to the card.
   Make the long straight edge of the paper
   even with the bottom of the card. The
   wavy edge should now overlap the green
   grass slightly.

6 Repeat steps 4 and 5 with the small piece
   of blue paper. Your card should now look
   like a pond with two sets of waves.

7 Tape the origami ducks anywhere you like
   on the blue water to complete your duck
   pond card.

24

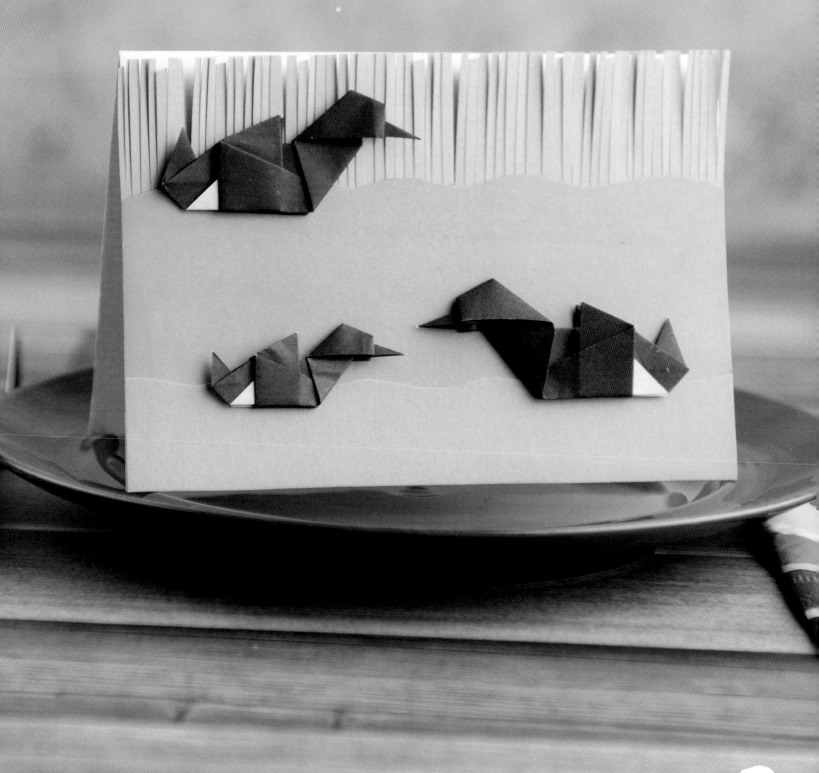

More crafting ideas

Variety is the spice of life...

Whoever said that every card you create in this chapter needs to be exactly the same? The more variety and imagination you apply to your greetings cards, the more fun they are to make and send. For instance, create the perfect Asian-themed invitation by using teacups and paper lanterns on the front of the card. Or add dimension to your duck pond by attaching accordion folded waves. Even the barnyard card has hidden potential when you add hayloft doors that open!

The card combinations you can come up with are endless – especially when you start using models in the chapters to come. Just imagine the amazing cards you can create with paper swans, finches, turtles and whales!

Origami ornaments

Finch

This simple bird looks like the finches seen hopping around bird feeders or perching on fences. Try out different double-sided papers to change the look of your origami finches.

1 Valley fold corner to corner and unfold.

2 Valley fold the edges to the centre.

3 Mountain fold the corner.

4 Valley fold the corners to the centre and unfold.

5 Squash fold the corners using the creases made in step 4.

6 Valley fold the points.

7 Valley fold the model in half.

8 Inside reverse fold the point to form a beak.

9 Pleat fold the tail.

10 Finished finch.

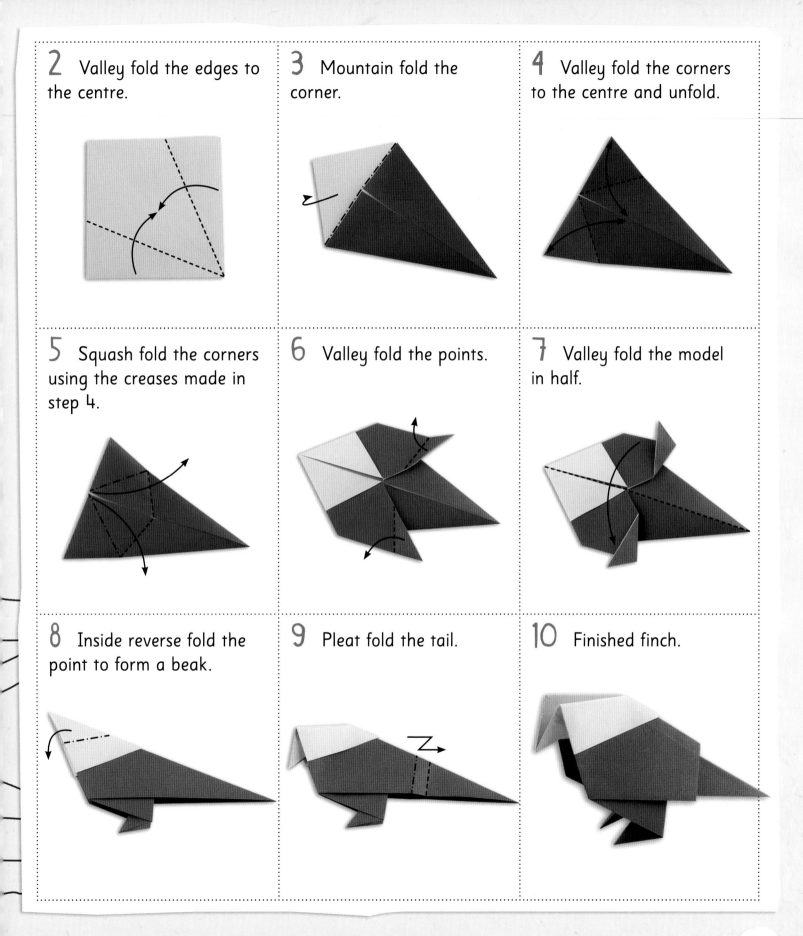

Bluebell

Bluebell stems droop under the weight of their beautiful blossoms. Fold a bouquet of these bell-shaped flowers to brighten someone's day.

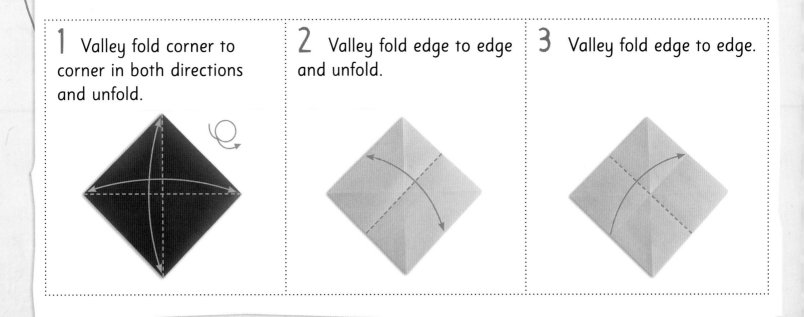

1 Valley fold corner to corner in both directions and unfold.

2 Valley fold edge to edge and unfold.

3 Valley fold edge to edge.

4 Squash fold.

5 Valley fold the top flaps to the centre. Repeat behind.

6 Valley fold the top flaps to the centre. Repeat behind.

7 Squash fold the top flaps. Repeat behind.

8 Mountain fold the top flaps. Repeat behind.

9 Curl the points down to make petals.

10 Push out the centre of the model with your finger.

11 Finished bluebell.

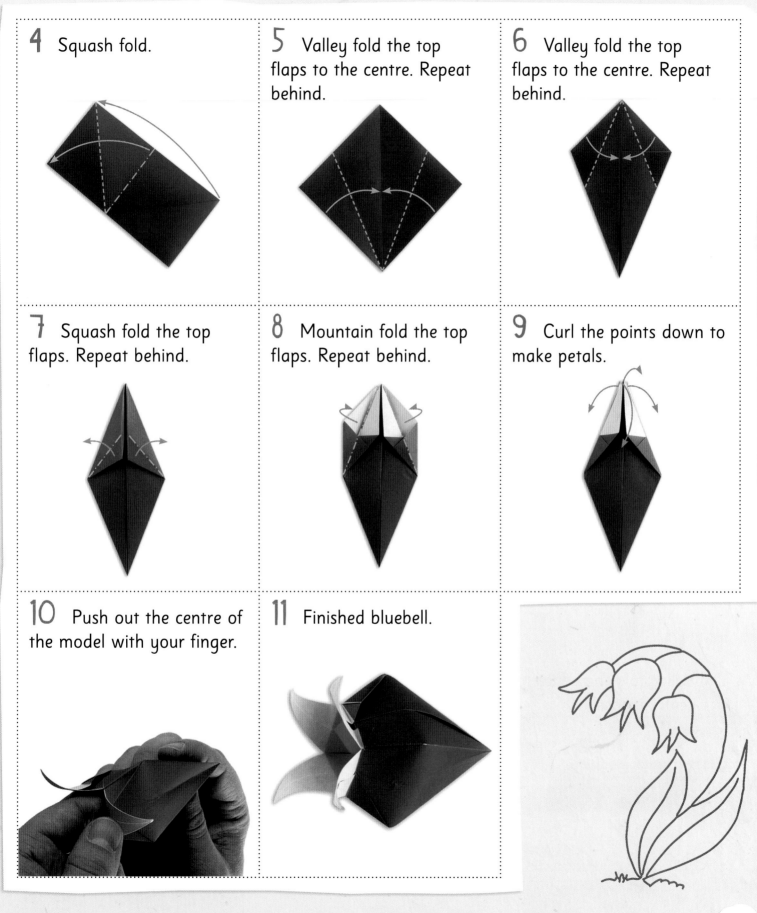

Ninja star

This four-point star looks like the throwing stars made famous by Japanese ninjas. Tap into your inner ninja with just two pieces of paper.

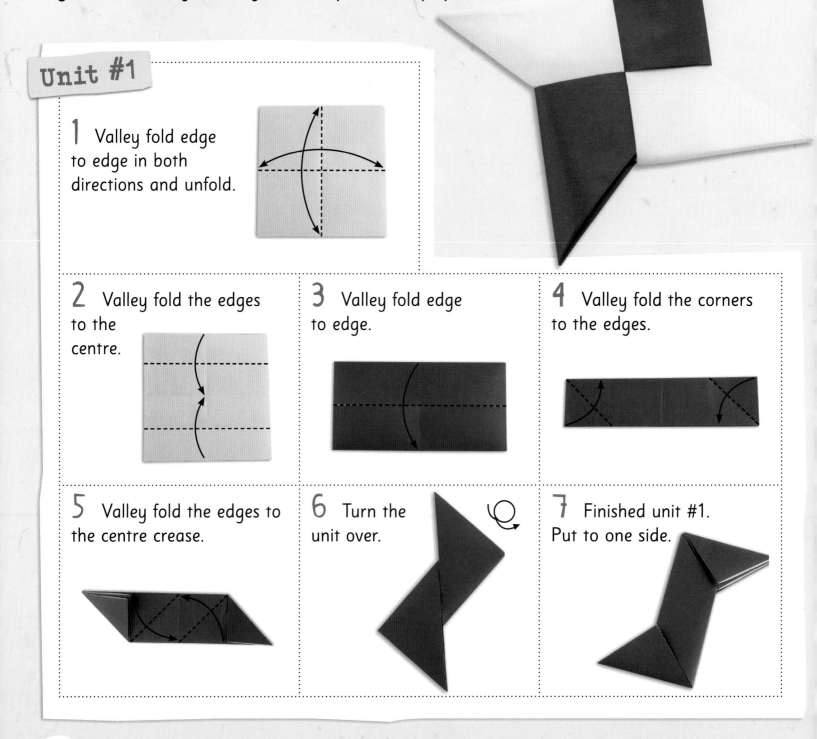

1 Valley fold edge to edge in both directions and unfold.

2 Valley fold the edges to the centre.

3 Valley fold edge to edge.

4 Valley fold the corners to the edges.

5 Valley fold the edges to the centre crease.

6 Turn the unit over.

7 Finished unit #1. Put to one side.

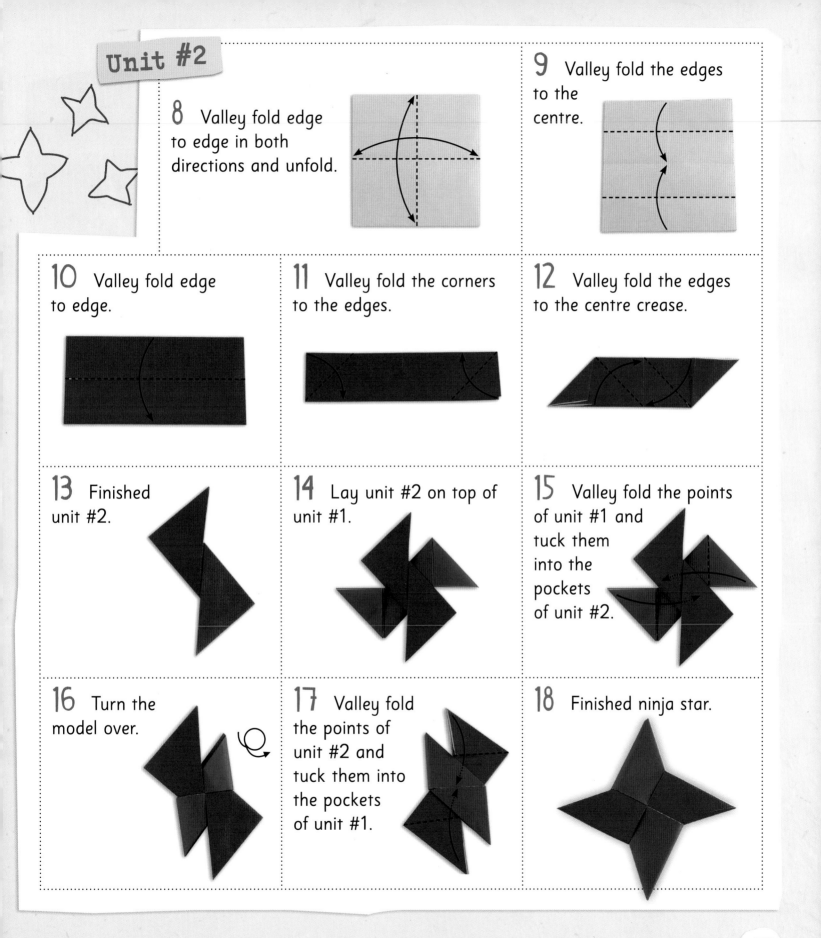

Unit #2

8 Valley fold edge to edge in both directions and unfold.

9 Valley fold the edges to the centre.

10 Valley fold edge to edge.

11 Valley fold the corners to the edges.

12 Valley fold the edges to the centre crease.

13 Finished unit #2.

14 Lay unit #2 on top of unit #1.

15 Valley fold the points of unit #1 and tuck them into the pockets of unit #2.

16 Turn the model over.

17 Valley fold the points of unit #2 and tuck them into the pockets of unit #1.

18 Finished ninja star.

Baubles and garland

Decorate any tree with an array of garlands and baubles. Origami bluebells, finches and ninja stars offer endless possibilities for wonderful hanging and perched ornaments.

What you need

scissors

origami ninja star

15-cm (6-in.) long
  piece of string

*fold the ninja star from
  15-cm (6-in.) squares

What you do

1 Cut a small notch out of the folded edge of one point of the ninja star. Make the notch slightly below the tip of the point.

2 Thread the string though the hole created by the notch.

3 Tie the ends of the thread into a knot. Pull the string so the knot hides inside the star's point.

4 Hang your ninja star ornament.

What you need

origami finch

craft glue

wooden clothes peg

*fold the finch from a
15-cm (6-in.) square

What you do

1 Spread the feet of the finch apart slightly.

2 Glue the clothes peg inside the centre of the finch. Position the clothes peg so it opens just below the finch's feet.

3 When the glue dries, clip your perched bird to a tree branch.

Bluebell garland

What you do

1 Cut small leaf shapes out of the green sheet of paper. Make twice as many leaves as you have bluebells.

2 Stretch out the string and space the bluebells evenly along its entire length.

3 With an adult's help, use hot glue to attach the points of each bluebell to the string. Finish each blossom by gluing a leaf to each side of each flower.

4 After the glue cools, hang the bluebell garland anywhere you like to add a touch of spring to any room.

What you need

scissors

sheet of green paper

4 or more origami bluebells

61-cm (24-in.) long or longer piece of string

hot glue gun

*fold the bluebells from 15-cm (6-in.) squares

Photo frame

Showcase your wallet-size photos with stunning photo frames. For the perfect size, fold this model with a 15-centimetre (6-inch) square of paper.

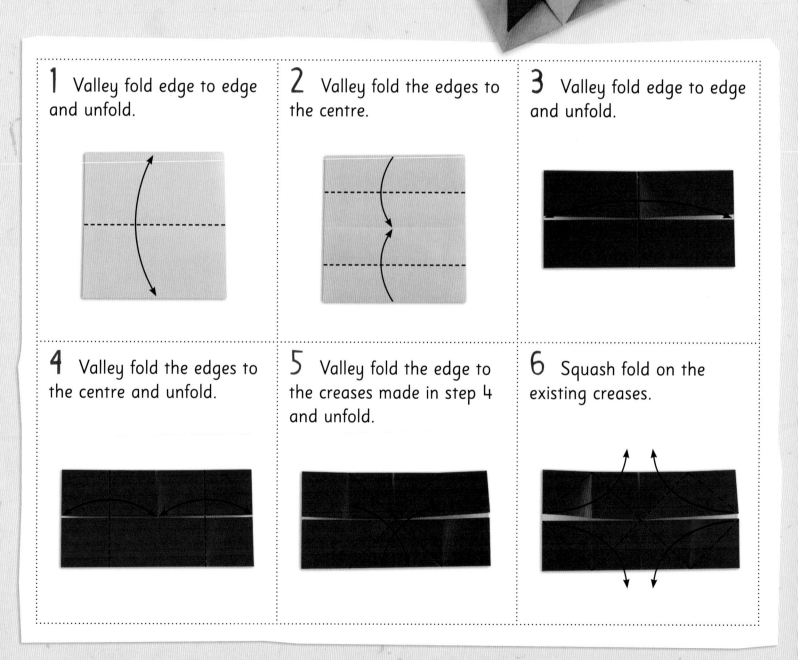

1 Valley fold edge to edge and unfold.

2 Valley fold the edges to the centre.

3 Valley fold edge to edge and unfold.

4 Valley fold the edges to the centre and unfold.

5 Valley fold the edge to the creases made in step 4 and unfold.

6 Squash fold on the existing creases.

7 Valley fold the inside edges of each flap to the centre.

8 Squash fold all four points.

9 Valley fold the edges of each of the four squares to their centre creases.

10 Squash fold all of the triangles.

11 Valley fold all four points.

12 Valley fold all four points.

13 Place a wallet-size photo inside the frame.

14 Finished photo frame.

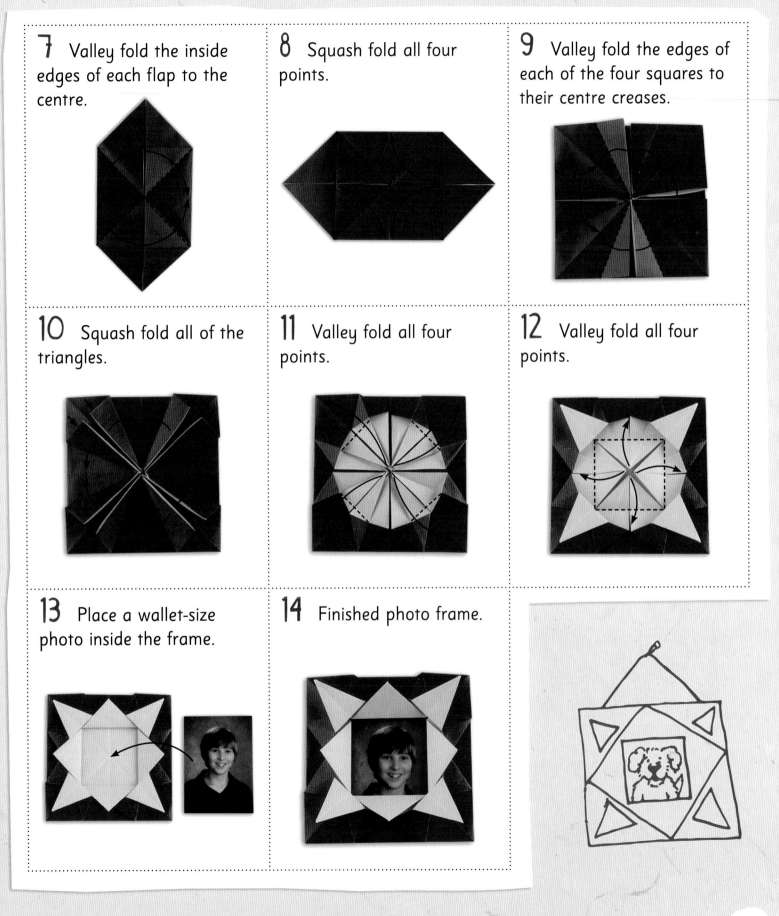

Photo frame ornament

Here's an ornament that looks great no matter which way the breeze blows. Front or back, this double-sided photo frame always shows you a face you adore.

What you need

2 origami photo frames

double-sided tape

2 wallet-size photos

30.5 cm (12-in.) long piece of string

*fold the photo frames from 15-cm (6-in.) squares

What you do

1 Decide how you would like your photo frames to line up and hang back-to-back. Frames could line up perfectly or be offset. They could also hang like a square or a diamond.

2 Tape the photos inside the frames based on the orientation you decided on in step 1. Put aside.

3 Tie the two ends of the string together in a knot.

4 Apply tape to the back of one photo frame. Place the knotted part of the string on the tape near the centre of the frame.

5 Place the back of the second photo frame on top of the tape and the string. Be sure the frames line up the way you decided in step 1 and press firmly.

6 Hang the ornament from a tree branch, a light fixture or anywhere it can turn freely.

Paper crane

The paper crane may be the most well-known origami model in the world. Legend says folding 1,000 of these paper birds brings good luck.

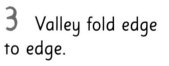

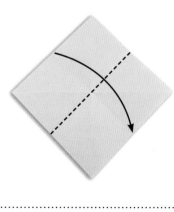

1 Valley fold corner to corner in both directions and unfold. Turn the paper over.

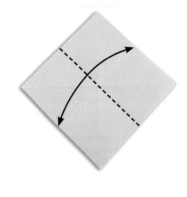

2 Valley fold edge to edge and unfold.

3 Valley fold edge to edge.

4 Squash fold.

5 Valley fold the top flaps to the centre and unfold. Repeat behind.

6 Inside reverse fold the top flaps. Repeat behind.

7 Valley fold the top flap. Repeat behind.

8 Valley fold the top flaps to the centre crease. Repeat behind.

9 Inside reverse fold the points upwards.

10 Inside reverse fold the point to make the head.

11 Gently pull the wings down and apart.

12 Finished crane.

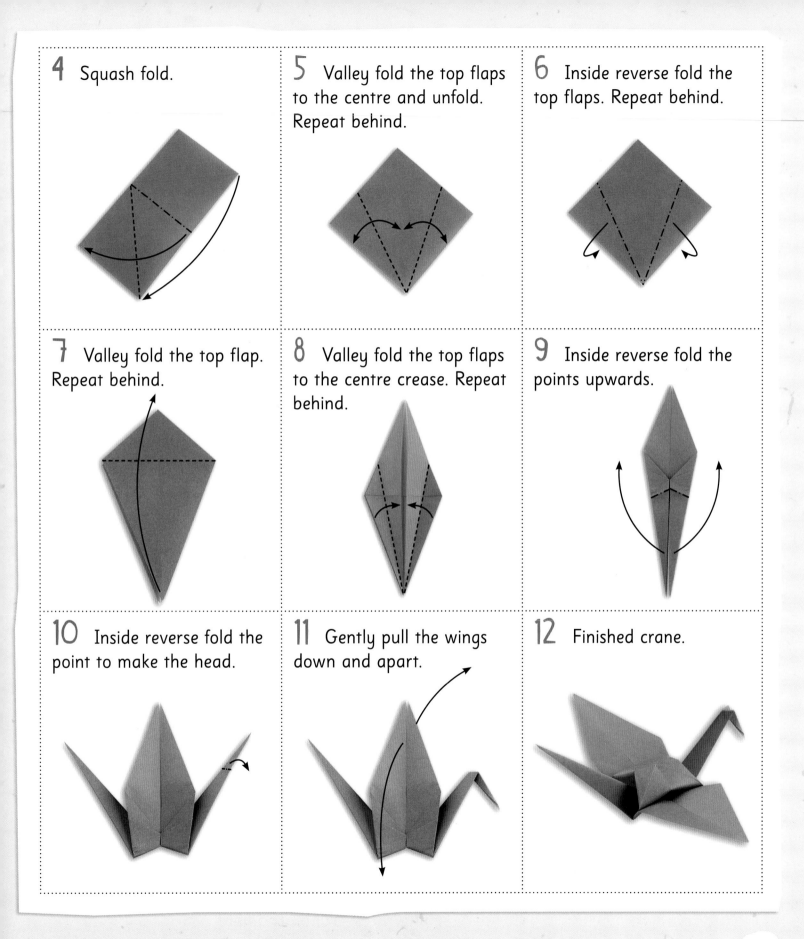

Three-crane ornament

Take origami ornaments to new heights! By simply threading classic paper cranes onto a string, you'll send them soaring. No matter where it hangs, this ornament will delight anyone who sees it!

What you need

51-cm (20-in.) long piece of string

3 origami cranes

large sewing needle

bead

*fold the cranes from 15-cm (6-in.) squares

What you do

1 Tie a loop in one end of the string.

2 Thread the other end of the string through the eye of the sewing needle.

3 Push the needle through the centre of an origami crane's back. Pull the needle and string out of the bottom of the crane.

4 Remove the needle and tie a knot just below the crane to hold it in place.

5 Repeat steps 2–4 with the other two cranes. Space the cranes evenly along the string.

6 Tie a bead on the end of the string to finish the three-crane ornament.

More crafting ideas

A gift worth giving...

If you're giving a gift, put your origami skills to good use. Many of the models in this book make excellent gift tags for any occasion. Flat models such as the cornflower, teacup and paper lantern are easy to write on and attach to any gift. You can also add dimension to bows and gift bags with butterflies, bluebells and paper cranes that pop off the packages.

No matter which models you use, the recipients of your gifts will "ooh" and "ahh" over your amazing gift tags. Best of all, the extra time you take making them will show just how much you really care.

Origami decorations

Butterfly

Butterflies come in countless colours and patterns. Take a hint from nature. Let your imagination run wild when picking colourful paper for this model.

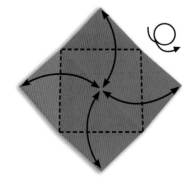

1 Valley fold edge to edge in both directions and unfold.

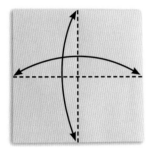

2 Valley fold corner to corner in both directions and unfold.

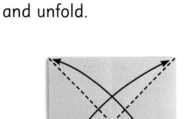

3 Valley fold the corners to the centre.

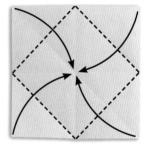

4 Turn the model over.

5 Valley fold the corners to the centre and unfold. Turn the model over.

6 Unfold the paper completely.

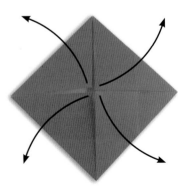

7 Valley fold the edges to the centre.

8 Squash fold the corners using the existing creases.

9 Mountain fold the model in half.

10 Valley fold the top flaps to the centre.

11 Valley fold the corners of the top flaps.

12 Valley fold the model in half.

13 Valley fold the top wing at a slight angle. Repeat behind.

14 Unfold the model halfway.

15 Finished butterfly.

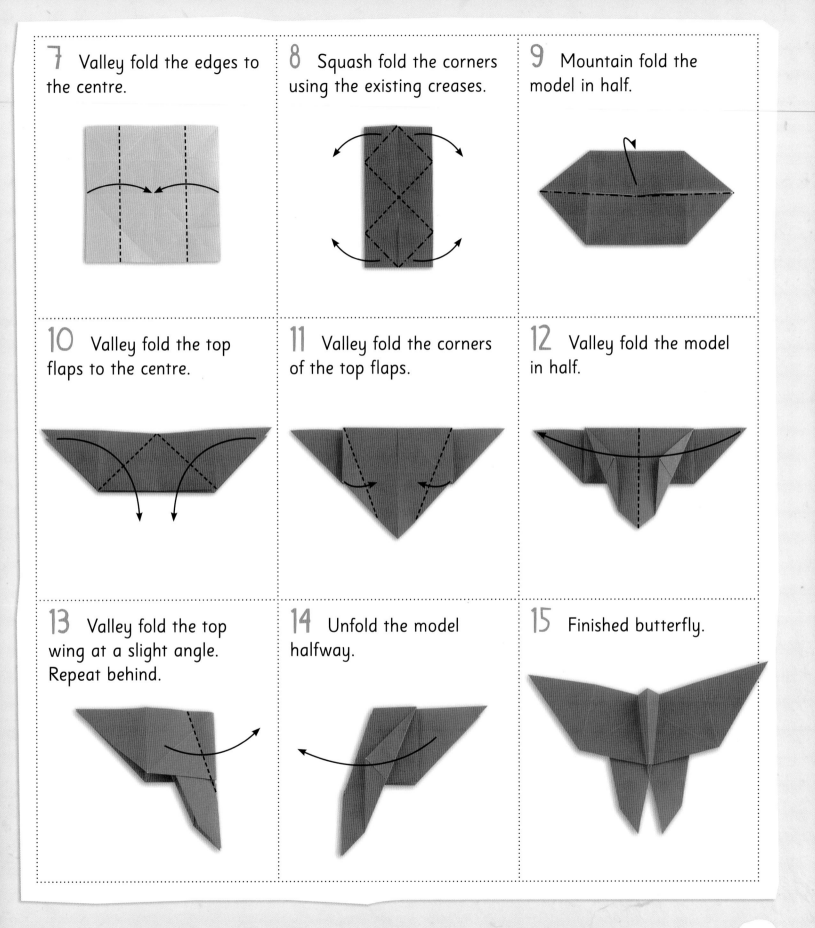

Butterfly magnet

Turn origami butterflies into magnets in no time flat! This quick and easy craft is the perfect decoration for refrigerators and school lockers.

What you need

craft glue

2 2.5-cm (1-in.) long pieces of stiff string or wire

origami butterfly

6 10.2-cm (4-in.) long pieces of yarn

small magnet

*fold the butterfly from a 15-cm (6-in.) square

What you do

1 Glue the stiff string or wire to the back of the butterfly's head to make antennae.

2 Glue the yarn to the butterfly's tail. Divide the yarn evenly between both sides of the tail.

3 Glue the small magnet to the centre of the butterfly's back.

4 Once the glue dries, stick your butterfly magnet to a refrigerator, locker or other metal surface.

★ Cube

Making an origami cube takes more than just nimble fingers. You'll inflate this model like a balloon with a puff of air.

1 Valley fold edge to edge in both directions and unfold. Turn the paper over.

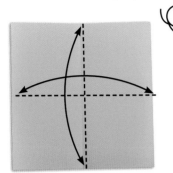

2 Valley fold corner to corner in both directions and unfold.

3 Squash fold the paper using the existing creases.

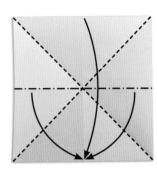

4 Valley fold the top flaps to the point. Repeat behind.

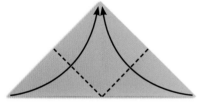

5 Valley fold the top flaps to the centre. Repeat behind.

6 Valley fold the top flaps to the centre. Repeat behind.

7 Valley fold and tuck the small triangles into the pockets. Repeat behind.

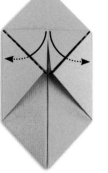

8 Spread the model's layers slightly and blow into the bottom hole to inflate.

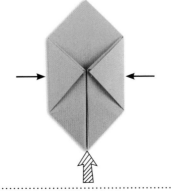

9 Finished cube.

Paper lanterns

Add pizzazz to any party with homemade paper lanterns. Just place a few origami cubes on a string of LED lights, and you're good to glow!

What you need

scissors

spool of string

string of LED lights

beads

spool of ribbon

origami cubes

*fold all origami cubes from
   15-cm (6-in.) squares

What you do

1 Cut a length of string slightly longer than the LED lights. Lay it parallel to the string of lights.

2 Slide beads onto the string and space them evenly along its length.

3 Tie one end of the string to one end of the lights.

4 Wrap the string around the light string. Work from the knot tied in step 3 to the end of the light string. Be sure to keep the beads evenly spaced as you go. Then tie off the loose end of the string.

5 Cut short strips of ribbon and tie them all along the light string. These ribbons will help hold the string and beads in place.

6 Push each LED light into the hole of an origami cube.

7 Plug in the light string and enjoy your glowing paper lanterns.

Swan

This simple swan is more than just a pretty bird. Its wings can open to hold your tiniest treasures.

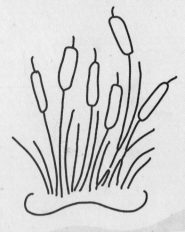

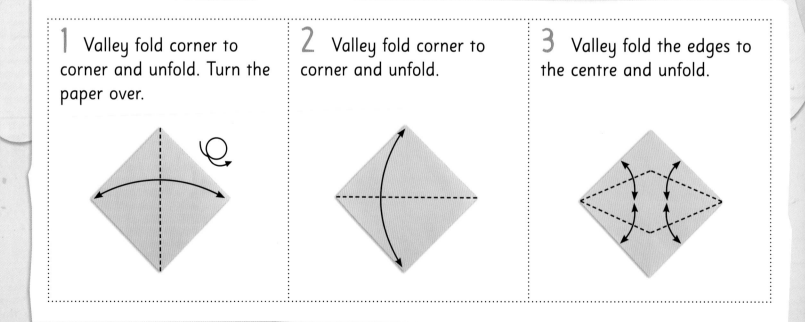

1 Valley fold corner to corner and unfold. Turn the paper over.

2 Valley fold corner to corner and unfold.

3 Valley fold the edges to the centre and unfold.

4 Rabbit ear fold on the creases made in step 3. At the same time, mountain fold the centre crease.

5 Valley fold both points. Allow the points to land about halfway between the corners and the left point.

6 Valley fold the points.

7 Mountain fold the model in half.

8 Pull the neck up and flatten.

9 Pull the head up and flatten.

10 Mountain fold the bottom point. Repeat behind.

11 Finished swan.

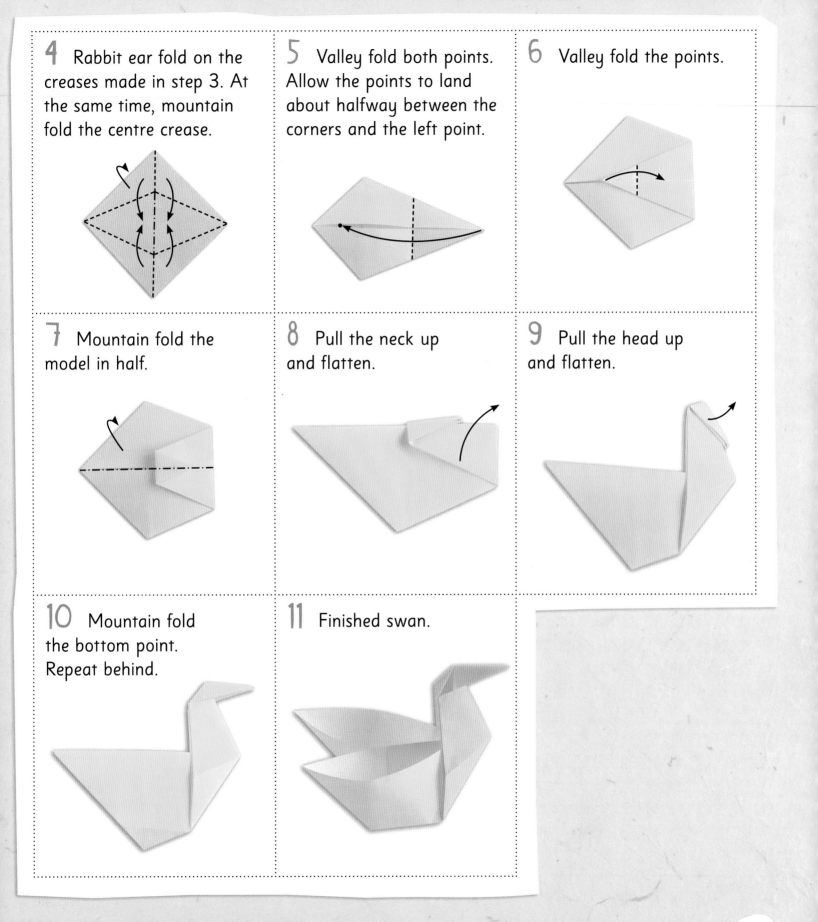

Tulip

Breathe life into this model with a puff of air. Then peel its petals to see how an origami tulip is born!

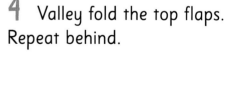

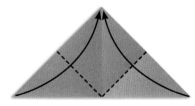

1 Valley fold edge to edge in both directions and unfold. Turn the paper over.

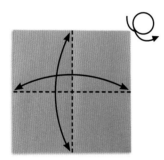

2 Valley fold corner to corner in both directions and unfold.

3 Squash fold the paper using the existing creases.

4 Valley fold the top flaps. Repeat behind.

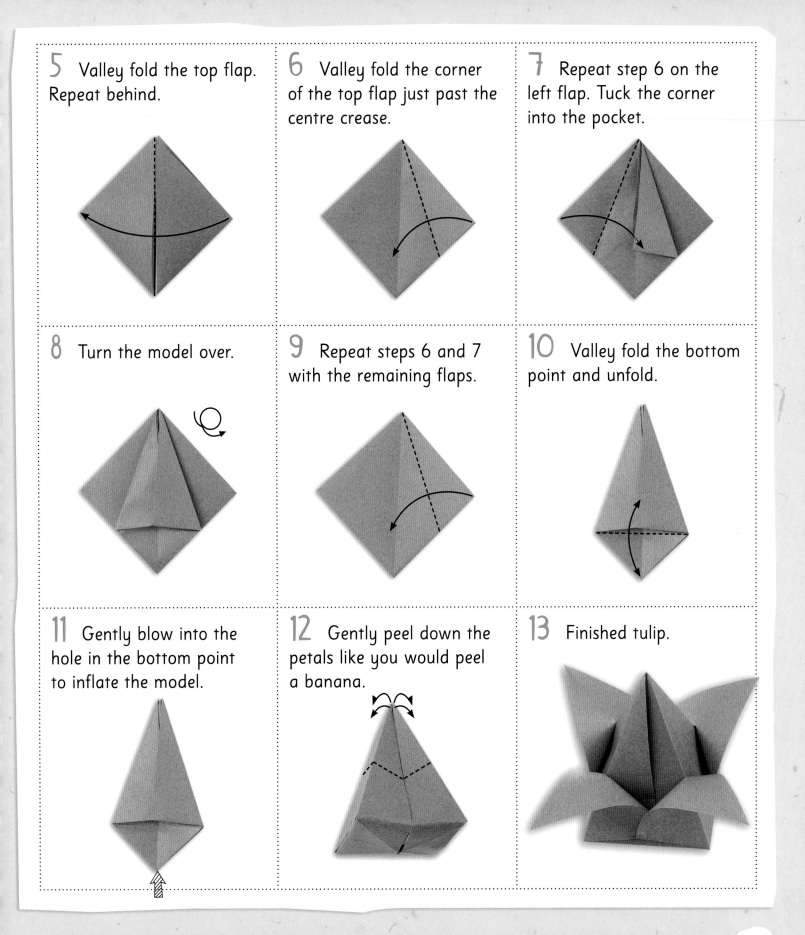

5 Valley fold the top flap. Repeat behind.

6 Valley fold the corner of the top flap just past the centre crease.

7 Repeat step 6 on the left flap. Tuck the corner into the pocket.

8 Turn the model over.

9 Repeat steps 6 and 7 with the remaining flaps.

10 Valley fold the bottom point and unfold.

11 Gently blow into the hole in the bottom point to inflate the model.

12 Gently peel down the petals like you would peel a banana.

13 Finished tulip.

Stem

Every origami flower looks better with a stem. Make your paper blossoms shine on this simple model.

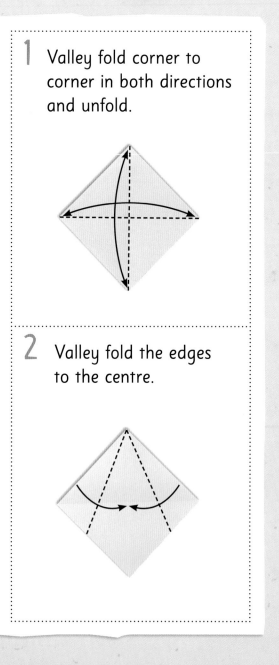

1 Valley fold corner to corner in both directions and unfold.

2 Valley fold the edges to the centre.

3 Valley fold the edges to the centre.

4 Valley fold the edges to the centre.

5 Valley fold point to point.

6 Valley fold the model in half.

7 Outside reverse fold the point.

8 Finished stem.

Springtime centrepiece

Decorate your table with a touch of spring. This clever centrepiece is blooming with style. And the sweet-filled swans will be a hit with all of your guests.

What you need

2 11- by 12.5-cm
(4.5- by 5-in.) pieces
of green card stock

scissors

5 small diamond-shaped
pieces of card stock

marker

30-cm (12-in.) long piece
of string

glue stick

2 origami stems

2 origami tulips

2 origami swans

assorted sweets

*fold all origami models from
15-cm (6-in.) squares

What you do

1 Fold a narrow flap on a long edge of each piece of green card stock. Stand the cards up on their flaps.

2 Cut long, narrow slits in the upright portion of both cards. Nest the cards to form a patch of grass. Place the grass in the centre of your table.

3 Fold the five diamond-shaped card stock pieces in half to form flags.

4 Write one letter on each flag to spell the word "PARTY".

5 Hang each flag on the string in order. Glue them in place. Put to one side.

6 Cut a notch near the tip of each origami stem. Make the notch on the straight edge of the stem directly above the leaf.

7 Thread the ends of the string through the holes created by the notches. Tie knots in the string to keep the ends from pulling out of the stems.

8 Place one stem on each side of the grass. Drape the flags over the grass in a way that pleases you.

9 Slide an origami tulip onto the tip of each stem.

10 Fill the wings of each origami swan with sweets. Place anywhere near the tulips and grass to complete your centrepiece.

More crafting ideas

Dare to make a scene...

Bring your origami models to life by placing them in clever scenes. With a little bit of sand, tiny paper turtles can imitate real baby sea turtles during their race to the waves. By crinkling some shiny wrapping paper and lining it with pebbles, you can fashion a pretty pond for your mandarin ducks. Even origami tulips and stems have presentation potential. Just plunk them into artificial grass bordered by a picket fence.

Whether you use your scenes for table centrepieces, dioramas for school projects or just for fun, your friends and family will be in awe of your origami creations. So don't be shy. Make a scene!

Origami scrapbooking

Animal finger puppets

Tap into your imagination with this simple animal finger puppet. Depending on how you fold the ears, it can look like a cat, a dog or even a pig.

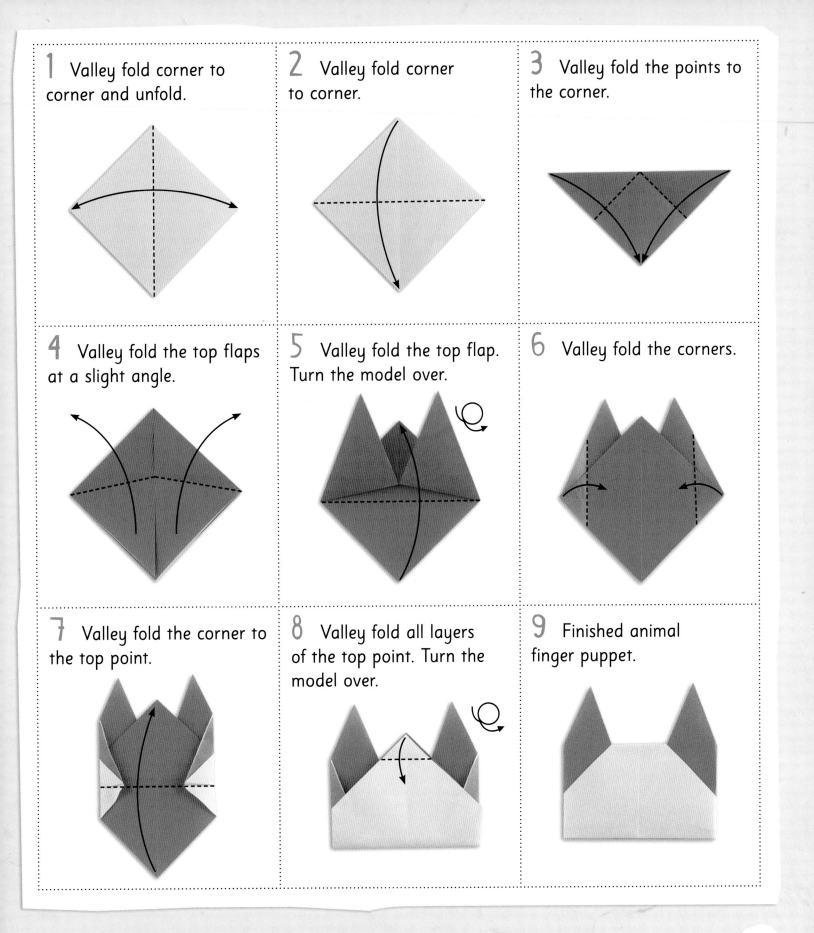

1 Valley fold corner to corner and unfold.

2 Valley fold corner to corner.

3 Valley fold the points to the corner.

4 Valley fold the top flaps at a slight angle.

5 Valley fold the top flap. Turn the model over.

6 Valley fold the corners.

7 Valley fold the corner to the top point.

8 Valley fold all layers of the top point. Turn the model over.

9 Finished animal finger puppet.

Animal hats scrapbook page

A scrapbook page is a great way to remember the good times and goofiness of friendship. Turn origami animal finger puppets into playful hats for your friends.

What you need

3 photos of your friends

2 or more origami animal finger puppets (hats)

scissors

coloured paper

30.5-cm (12-in.) square scrapbook page

double-sided tape

*fold finger puppets from 9-cm (3.5-in.) squares

What you do

1 Pick one photo for the animal hats. It should show your friends large enough that the hats will fit them well.

2 Trim around the edges of the people in the photo you've selected. Put to one side.

3 Cut coloured paper into strips and rectangles that are slightly larger than the photos. Also cut out letters to spell words such as "FRIENDS" or "CLASSMATES".

4 Arrange your photos on the scrapbook page in a way that pleases you. Use the paper strips and rectangles as decorations and borders behind the photos. Place any words you cut out wherever they look best.

5 When everything is where you want it, tape all of the photos, borders, decorations and letters in place on the scrapbook page.

6 Place the animal hats on top of the photos of the friends you trimmed around in step 2. Tape the hats in place to finish your friendship page.

Whale

Thar she blows! Blue whales are giants of the sea. Make your paper versions large or small in any colour you like.

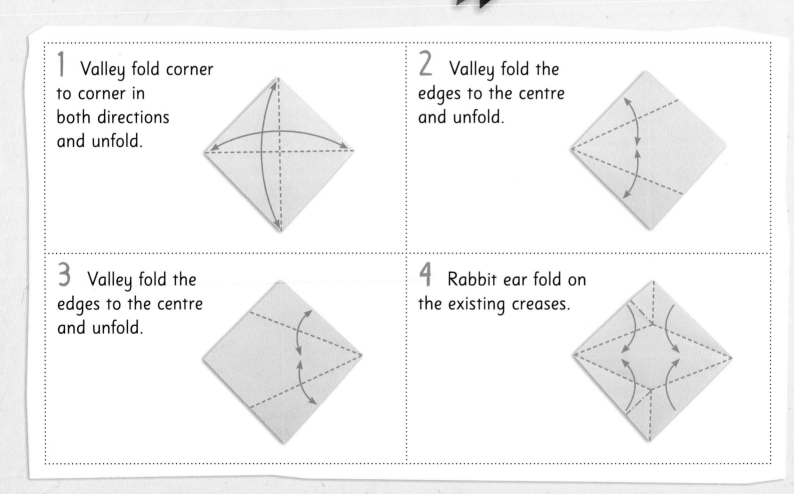

1 Valley fold corner to corner in both directions and unfold.

2 Valley fold the edges to the centre and unfold.

3 Valley fold the edges to the centre and unfold.

4 Rabbit ear fold on the existing creases.

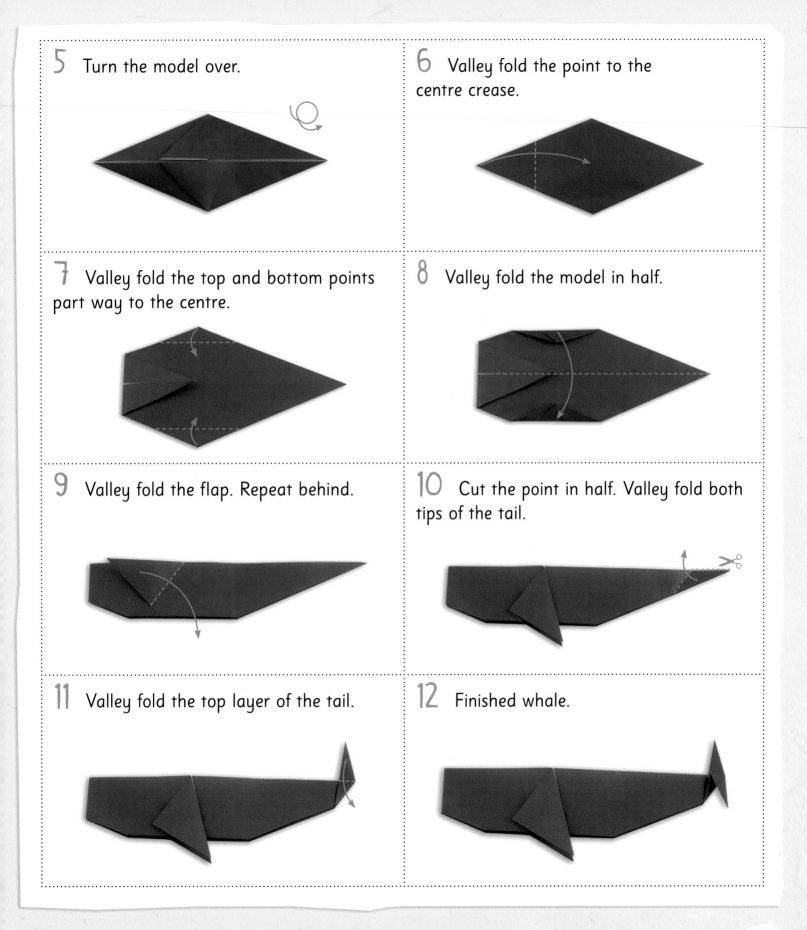

5 Turn the model over.

6 Valley fold the point to the centre crease.

7 Valley fold the top and bottom points part way to the centre.

8 Valley fold the model in half.

9 Valley fold the flap. Repeat behind.

10 Cut the point in half. Valley fold both tips of the tail.

11 Valley fold the top layer of the tail.

12 Finished whale.

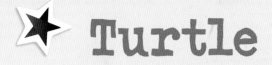

Turtle

As soon as they hatch, baby sea turtles scamper across the beach and into the ocean. Fold dozens of tiny turtles to create your own race to the waves.

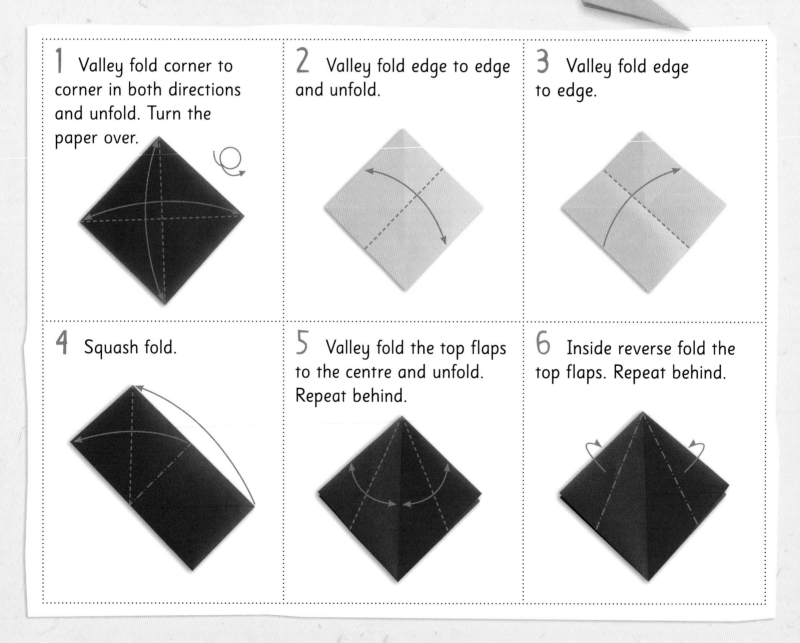

1 Valley fold corner to corner in both directions and unfold. Turn the paper over.

2 Valley fold edge to edge and unfold.

3 Valley fold edge to edge.

4 Squash fold.

5 Valley fold the top flaps to the centre and unfold. Repeat behind.

6 Inside reverse fold the top flaps. Repeat behind.

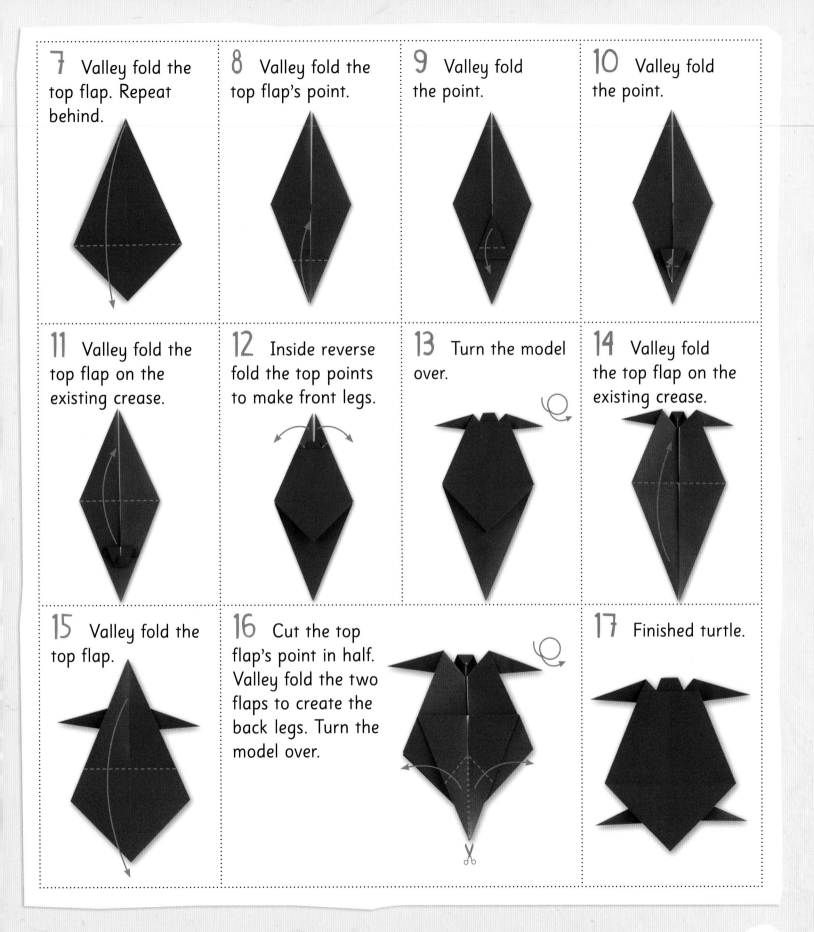

7 Valley fold the top flap. Repeat behind.

8 Valley fold the top flap's point.

9 Valley fold the point.

10 Valley fold the point.

11 Valley fold the top flap on the existing crease.

12 Inside reverse fold the top points to make front legs.

13 Turn the model over.

14 Valley fold the top flap on the existing crease.

15 Valley fold the top flap.

16 Cut the top flap's point in half. Valley fold the two flaps to create the back legs. Turn the model over.

17 Finished turtle.

Under-the-sea scrapbook page

Save the memories of your latest trip to the beach with an under-the-sea scrapbook page. Origami whales and turtles will help you capture the fun above and below the water.

What you need

3 or more photos

30.5-cm (12-in.) square scrapbook page

scissors

coloured paper

origami whale

3 small origami turtles

double-sided tape

self-adhesive gemstones

*fold the whale from a 15-cm (6-in.) square and the turtles from 5- to 10-cm (2- to 4-in.) squares

What you do

1 Arrange the photos on the scrapbook page in a way that pleases you. If necessary, cut off any photo edges that have people or scenery you don't want to see.

2 Cut coloured paper into strips and rectangles that are slightly larger than the photos. Place them behind the photos as borders.

3 Arrange the whale and turtles so they look like they are swimming around the photos.

4 When everything is where you want it, tape all of the photos, borders and origami in place.

5 Stick gemstones around the page to give your underwater scene a little extra sparkle.

Cornflower

Cornflowers burst like stars into brilliant shades of light blue. With four points bursting outwards, this origami blossom looks great in any colour.

1 Valley fold corner to corner in both directions and unfold. Turn the paper over.

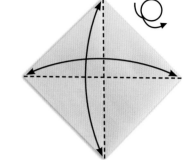

2 Valley fold edge to edge and unfold.

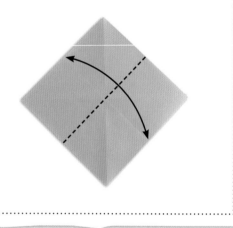

3 Valley fold edge to edge.

4 Squash fold.

5 Valley fold the top flaps to the centre and unfold. Repeat behind.

6 Squash fold on the creases made in step 5. Repeat behind.

7 Valley fold the top flap. Repeat behind.

8 Squash fold. Repeat behind.

9 Valley fold the top layer while squash folding the inside points.

10 Squash fold the points to form petals.

11 Finished cornflower.

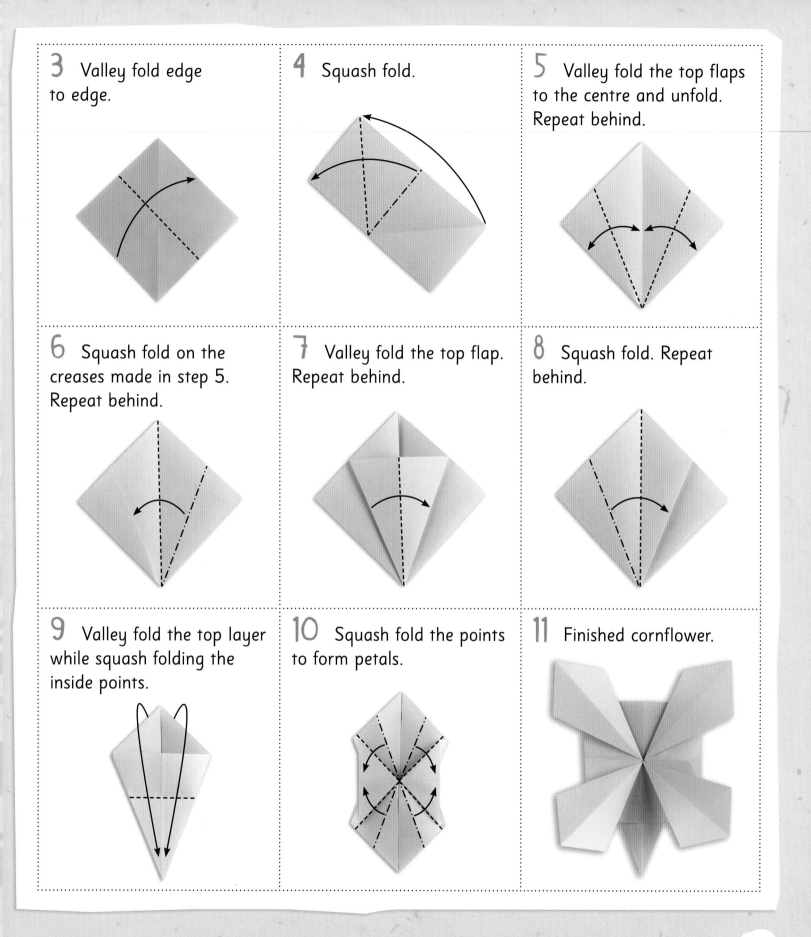

Camellia

Camellias are flowering trees and shrubs. More than 3,000 types of camellias bloom around the world.

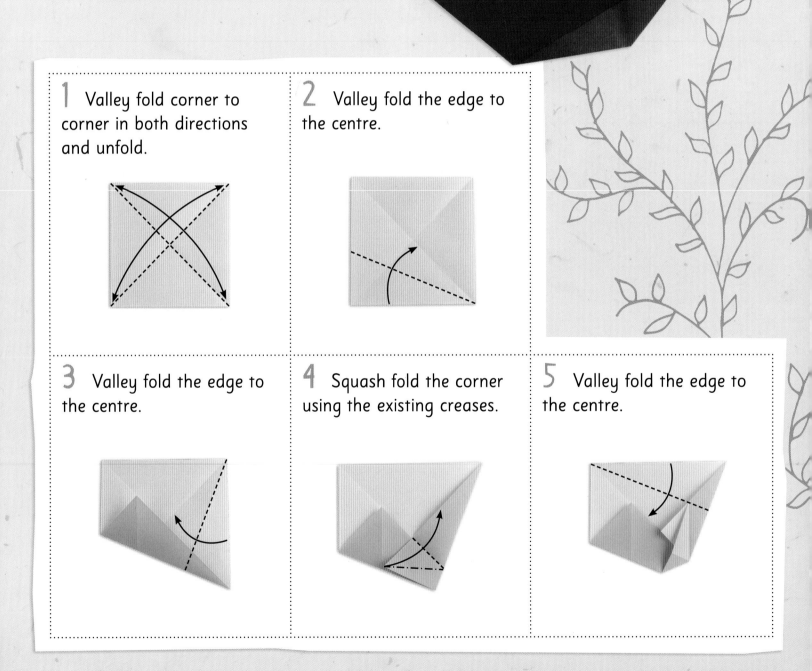

1 Valley fold corner to corner in both directions and unfold.

2 Valley fold the edge to the centre.

3 Valley fold the edge to the centre.

4 Squash fold the corner using the existing creases.

5 Valley fold the edge to the centre.

6 Squash fold the corner using the existing creases.

7 Valley fold the corner to the dot.

8 Squash fold the corner using the existing creases.

9 Valley fold the top flap.

10 Pull the lower layer of paper to the front.

11 Squash fold the corner using the existing creases.

12 Valley fold the flap and tuck it into the pocket.

13 Tuck the flap into the pocket.

14 Finished camellia.

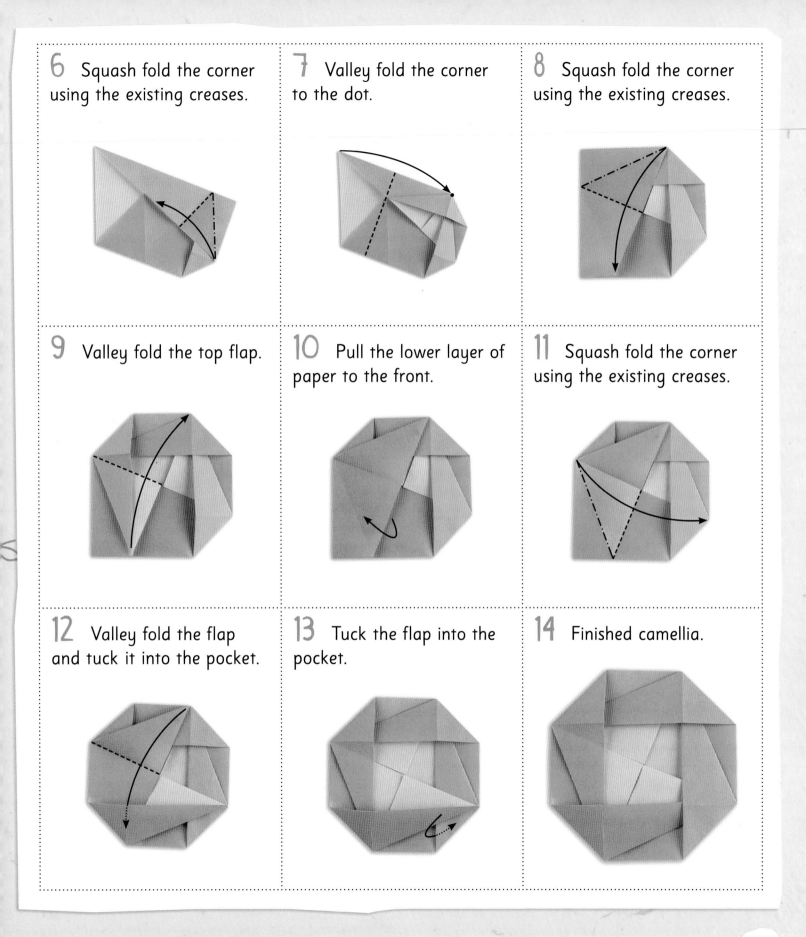

Floral scrapbook page

A simple floral-themed scrapbook page is the perfect way to capture a summer picnic in the park. Make paper leaves to serve as frames for your photos. Then add a few origami blossoms for just the right burst of colour.

What you need

scissors

3 or more photos

2 22- by 28-cm (8.5- by 11-in.) sheets of green paper

30.5-cm (12-in.) square scrapbook page

origami cornflower

2 origami camellias

double-sided tape

*fold all origami flowers from 15-cm (6-in.) squares

What you do

1 Cut curves around opposite corners of the photos to shape each one like a leaf.

2 Place the photos on the green paper. Cut around the photos, leaving a little bit of extra room on all sides, to make slightly larger leaf shapes. These leaves will serve as frames for your photos.

3 Arrange the photos and leaves on the scrapbook page in a way that pleases you.

4 Place one origami flower near each photo.

5 Cut long, thin strips of green paper to serve as stems. Arrange the stems so they connect to the flowers and leaves.

6 When everything is where you want it, tape all of the photos, leaves, stems and origami in place.

7 Trim off the ends of any stems that meet the edges of the scrapbook page to complete the craft.

More crafting ideas

Play with papers and sizes . . .

Whether you're folding a single model or creating an elaborate origami craft, be creative with your choice of paper. Origami paper comes in a huge variety of colours, patterns and textures. Sometimes an unexpected colour or pattern can make a model truly shine in the finished craft. And don't just limit yourself to origami paper. You can use wrapping paper, paper bags and even tin foil to make your models.

In addition to paper selection, don't forget to experiment with paper sizes. After all, what's cuter than miniature origami folded from tiny squares of paper? Or more impressive than huge models that dominate a table or room? And you never know, sometimes folding models in different sizes helps them work together in unexpected ways.

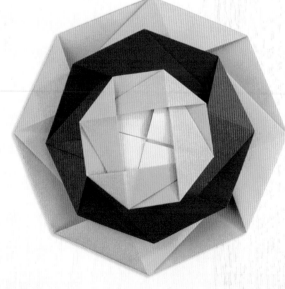

Explore more

Find more great origami and craft books on the Raintree website: *www.raintree.co.uk*

About the author

Christopher Harbo has a passion for origami. He began folding paper 12 years ago when he tried making a simple model for his nephews. With that first successful creation, he quickly became hooked on the art form. He ran to his local library and borrowed every origami book he could find to increase his folding skills. Today he continues to develop his origami skills and loves the thrill of folding new creations.
In addition to traditional origami and its many uses, he also enjoys folding paper aeroplanes and modular origami.
When he's not folding paper, Christopher spends his free time reading Japanese manga and watching movies.